♪ **First Melodies** ♫

www.firstmelodies.com

Melody Sings About Magic

Written & Illustrated by Kirsty Clinch

This book belongs too

....

Dedicated to
Phil Glasson

Hello, I'm Melody, I sing, dance and play.
I live in a land not too far away.
I go on adventures and have lots of fun,
and sing songs to everyone.
Today we are making our dreams come true.
Magic is inside all of you.

Hello, I'm Melody, how are you?
Can you see that magic fairy door?
If you are happy sad or unsure,
write it down on some paper,
And leave your note at the door.
"Look a fairy!"

The Fairy Song

I'm a little fairy, I am very small,
but my fairy wings protect me and
the magic dust I store.
If you ring a bell, near my door.
Leave a little note if you feel
sad or unsure.
Do you need my help,
with anything at all?
I'll do my best to help you,
Ring your bells.

(♪)

So sing, la la oo oo ee ee ah ah.
La la oo oo ee ee ah ah.
And ring the bell near my little door,
Because that is my magic fairy call.
Sing, la la oo oo ee ee ah ah.
Sing la la oo oo ee ee ah ah.

Hello, I'm Melody, how are you?
There's something inside my pocket that you cannot ignore.
It's tinier than expected,
But it can still go ROAR!
Sometimes the best things in life can be really small.
"Look it's a dinosaur!"

The Dinosaur Song

There's a dinosaur in my pocket.
There's a dinosaur in my pocket.
I'm not telling lies I promise you he's right inside.
There's a dinosaur in my pocket.

There's a dinosaur in my pocket.
There's a dinosaur in my pocket.
One day I'll have more
and they'll be the best of friends.
1, 2, 3, 4, 5, 6, 7!

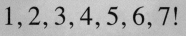

(x2)

Hello, I'm Melody, how are you?
Have you been into the magic woods before?
A wonder awaits us, it's rare and unique.
Just like each and every-one of you,
who is reading my book. "Look a unicorn!"

The Unicorn Song

I look like a horse, but I am not of course.
I'm extremely rare,
there's something about me.
I am unique,
but everyone knows me of course.
I'm a unicorn,
with a rainbow spiral horn.

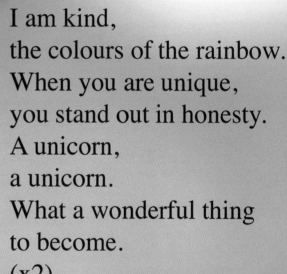

I am kind,
the colours of the rainbow.
When you are unique,
you stand out in honesty.
A unicorn,
a unicorn.
What a wonderful thing
to become.
(x2)

Hello. I'm Melody, how are you?
How many magical words do you know?
I have a friend that can cast some spells.
Using some magical words as well.
"Look, it's Harry the Wizard!"

Harry The Wizard Song.

I'm Harry the wizard.
I like to cast spells for everything but love,
Because love is inside you.
You don't need a spell to be loved.
L L L L L Loved (x4)

I'm Harry the wizard.
I only cast spells to help someone in need.
If they're hungry or feel sad.
I can give a warm hug and they know they are loved.
L L L L L Loved (x4)

(x2)

Hello, I'm Melody, how are you?
Magic can also be the things that make you, you.
You may have a talent, a big kid heart.
A different hair colour, or a different head start.
But that's what makes us extra special.
And that is magic, when being truly you.
"Look a little confident mouse!"

The Little Mouse Song.

I'm a little tiny mouse,
With a really big toe.
But it really doesn't matter,
Because it makes me really cool.
It gives me extra power.
Have a look at what I can do!

I'm a little tiny mouse,
With a really big nose.
But it really doesn't matter,
Because it makes me really cool.
It gives me extra power.
Have a look at what I can do!

Hello, I'm Melody, how are you?
Have you been to the seaside before?
Look straight ahead, out to the waves.
Magic lives deep down, right past those caves.
I like being me, but if I had to choose.
I'd be me as a mermaid, so I could explore the ocean.
"Look some mermaids!"

The Mermaid Song

Why would I want to be anyone else but me? (x2)
But if I could I'd be me as a mermaid.
Swimming in the sea and singing to the ocean beneath me.
I wouldn't have to do my hair or worry about what to wear.
As a mermaid, as a mermaid.

My scales would shine, and I would smile.
I'd just be singing in the deep blue sea.
As a mermaid, as a mermaid.
(x2)

Hello, I'm Melody, how are you?
Have you ever felt different,
been bullied or felt confused?
Remember one shoe size, is not made for all.
Words can be painful but be true to yourself.
Your values matter, you're worthy and you're loved.
"Look it's Phil the dragon, and he is always himself."

Phil The Dragon Song

Phil the dragon, he was always scared.
Because he danced all night and day.
He was afraid of what the others might say,
Because dragons breathe fire all day.

But Phil the dragon had a heart of gold,
And he only breathed fire for warmth.
All he wanted was to smile and dance,
And to make other dragons laugh.
Because Phil the dragon,
Is the best dragon that we have.

(X2)

Hello, I'm Melody, how are you?
Do any of my friends play the ukulele?
I like to sing, play the guitar and the ukulele too.
This ukulele is special and can make dreams come true.
"Look my magic ukulele!"

The Magic Ukulele Song.

G C E A
G C E A
The magic notes on my ukulele.

G C E A
G C E A
These are the open strings I like to play.

G is for growing up and trying my best.
C is for crying when I need a rest.
E is for everyone I love and respect.
A is for appreciating that I can breathe.

G is for getting sleep that I may need.
C is for clapping others that succeed.
E is for every time I put my needs first.
A is for always loving those in need. (x2)

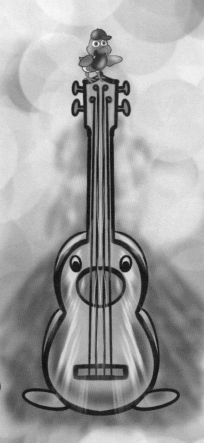

G C E A
G C E A
The magic notes on my ukulele.

G C E A
G C E A
These are the open strings I like to play.

Ok, goodbye from Melody.
It's been such a wonderful day.
Maybe tomorrow we can sing, dance, play,
and go on another adventure like today.

I'll see you soon,
keep smiling bright.
One more song, and then it's goodbye,
Goodnight!

The Magic Song.

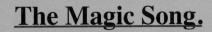

Don't you love sunny days?
When people smile and laugh and play.
But when you know it's safe to cry,
Because sometimes magic can die.

Let's talk to friends and family.
If we are feeling scared and unsure.
Hopefully we can build ourselves up again,
Even if it's slow.

Remember the four magic words,
Please and thank you.
You're welcome, I'm sorry!
Always be kind and help those in need.
Yet most of all, take time to love you.

Be kind to yourself, and love yourself,
And then not forgetting everyone else.

Kirsty Clinch is the founder
of the music school
First Melodies, in
Wiltshire, England

www.firstmelodies.com

Music is her passion, and as a qualified nursery nurse,
well-known professional singer/songwriter,
music teacher, and author,
Kirsty has put all her skills together to make interactive,
funny and educational music based books that accompany her YouTube channel,
First Melodies.
So, you can read, have fun and sing along with your little ones with the help of
Kirsty, always.
Melody is the interactive mascot at First Melodies.

Find all the songs to accompany this book, and the first and second book of this
series, Melody sings at the zoo and Melody sings about transport,
at the music school & YouTube channel, @firstmelodies.

Kirsty would like to thank you for your patience in waiting for the 3rd book.
As since opening the official music school of First Melodies,
finding the time to complete this has been hard.
I appreciate you personally, for sticking around
and still interacting & purchasing my books.

Winner of the Small Business Sunday Award.

With Special thanks to
My family and friends
for all the support.

With Special thanks to
Emily, for the help with the
final book reading.

With special thanks to Skeet,
for spreading the word in America
and for donating to the school.

Printed in Great Britain
by Amazon